Seedling

The Youngest Years

The debut account in the inspirational
Relinquish & Reap Series

by

Jessica Janna

&

April Alisa Marquette

April Rain Books
ꝺꝺꝺ

Seedling
© Copyright 2009 by Jessica Janna & April Alisa Marquette
Edited by Romesia Stevenson
rcds31@yahoo.com

ISBN   978-1-61539-572-9

Printed in the United States of America

Some of the names in this narrative have been changed.

Visit the author at www.aprilalisamarquette.com
Library of Congress Catalog Card No.: On File

For Cleopatra ... Jessica's mother, April's grandmother...

Our *goddess of hearth, home, and heart —you taught us, with minimal words, to worship*

I will instruct thee and teach thee in the way,

which thou shalt go: I will guide thee with mine eye.

Psalms 32:8

Forward

**Memories come unsolicited ... and often in no
particular order**

*Dear reader, not only is Jessica Janna a singer,
songwriter, and recording artist, she is also my
mother. A woman of incalculable talent, she is a
renowned evangelist, and motivational speaker.
Truly selfless, Jessica has long been a loving
mentor for many.*

*As a child, Jessica picked cotton in the heat of the
day, with her mother. Thus, at her mother's side,
she learned to walk with God.*

*From her father, Jessica garnered her love of song,
and musical abilities.*

*Having attended theological seminary when I was a
girl, Jessie served as the Co-Pastor of a Queens
New York Church. Once known as the Songbird of
the East, she also headlined in concert at New
York's Prestigious Carnegie Hall. No stranger to
the stage, she has worked with many a jazz great. A
priestess in the truest sense of the word, Jessica has
provided a home for, and has helped, many.*

*A genuine friend and teacher, Jessica is proudest of
her achievements as a mother.*

I will also inform you, dear reader that Jess, my mother, got a little snippy during the penning of this—Seedling. I suppose my plying her with questions, for clarity, raised her dander... However, she and I persevered, and are proud to offer you her precious gift.

My mother offers the gift of her self, her memories, and wisdom gained. Opening her life and heart, it is her hope that in some way, you, dear reader, will benefit from her story, from her seventy years upon God's green earth.

It is my prayer that my mother's offering, told in this, the first of seven volumes, will bless you.

Sincerely,

April Alisa Marquette

Table of Contents

Table of Contents
Continued

Twin Seeds

*J*ESSE Lee - he was born first.

*J*ESSICA Janna - she followed, minutes later, the seventh child of eleven.

*T*HUS began what has become an extraordinary life of change and movement…

Jessica Janna & April Alisa Marquette

*J*ESSICA (Jessie) recalls:

I must have been about three or four. My twin
was gone, deceased at mere months. It had been
said; the midwife cut his umbilical cord too short,
thus shortening my twin brother's life. Such
happened in those days.

Therefore, on the particular day of which I now speak, my mother and father had gone to work, and I had been left with the lady who kept me during the day.

I do not remember where the day lady was. I only remember that I was *drawn* outside.

That is the only way I can describe it.

It was as if something out of doors serenely called to something within me. That bigger something, and light, like I had not seen before, drew little me. This light appeared, inside, and I followed it out of the back door of our flat.

Barefoot, I stepped out and onto the plateau of the mountain on which we lived. I looked up...

It seemed as though the descending clouds were so low that they were attainable. I watched as slowly, they enveloped me.

Jessica Janna & April Alisa Marquette

They did not cover my head, nor was I afraid, but this near-mist wrapped around me, and felt somewhat cool to the touch.

I recall standing there, a little brown girl, knowing somewhere deep within that this was surreal, although many years would pass before I would learn that word.

I believe *that* was my first spiritual experience. Or if not, it is the very first that I can recall.

I also remember the mountain plateau on which I'd stood. My brown legs and feet were bare, beneath my little dress that was nothing special.

Even today, more than sixty-some years later, yet I remember the drop-down into the valley. I remember once I'd been allowed to peek. My dad, a slender brown man held me safe while I glanced over.

I do not remember if we were in Tennessee, or someplace different, perhaps because at the time I was too young, not yet cognizant of such things. I only remember, after seventy years, that the day lady called me ... back, from that surreal spiritual experience, the one that I consider my first.

Now, I can remember nothing else, not in the moments just before, or after, that occurrence.

Jessica Janna & April Alisa Marquette

Song & Dream

JESSICA (Jessie) recalls:

SONG was my first strength, along with faith—a belief in change, and movement.

I know I inherited cadence and music from my father. From my mother I garnered belief. It was what she taught, but more importantly, it was what, and how, she lived.

A woman of few words, Mother, whose given name was Cleopatra—Ms. Cleo to most who knew her—was what today would be known as a mover and a shaker.

Mother was beautiful, brown, a lithe, willowy woman, who worked hard. I remember her doing many different types of work during my formative years. She also cooked *so*, until eating, you would hurt yourself because her food was so tasty! And though she loved my father, a slender man with a congenial open look and soulful brown eyes, she left him.

Mother moved and shook—the dust off of her feet whenever she left any place, or anyone, because there were just some things she would not take; but that is another recollection for another time...

However, before Mother left my father, with us (her babies) in tow, I encountered Song.

My father sang. With his melodious rich voice, the song just seemed to swell up and cascade out of him, and it called to me. It must have actually done so long before I became aware of it, because nearly all my life Song has bubbled up and out of me too.

Way back, Song gave character and shape to my unknown self. I believe the precious gift of song recognized *me*, the very soul of me, even when I was just a hint of a girl.

My genuine self, the subconscious me, then embraced, without my conscious knowledge, the path that had already been designed expressly for me.

Therefore, when Mother took me places, others recognized the song in me. People acknowledged the talent, the gift, which emanated from within me.

Ah, there was a song; *I Know the Lord Has Laid His Hands on me…* I was quite small at the time, but I recall. Mother had placed us in school in Memphis, Tennessee.

The music teacher there taught us many things, among them, Negro Spirituals, and at one point, he needed a lead for a song. We were to sing it, he informed us, in an upcoming school production.

Those were big back then. Anyway, I do not remember how I got involved, and wound up with the part. I was to lead the *Hands on Me* song.

As small as I was, the song rose and swelled inside me. It trilled up and out, and I was happy to release it. People tapped their feet, and patted their hands as Song took hold of me, used me to bring joy.

Later, it became apparent that some students were enthralled with the little girl who oh so properly sang *The Lord Has Laid His* (I pronounced it 'honds') *Hands on Me.* Others found my diction quite amusing. Then my poor elder sister, she wound up getting many a good-natured teasing about me and my singing.

However, with Mother moving and shaking, out of necessity, I remember singing in Moscow, Arkansas. We called it Mos-Cow, no Mos-Coe. I also sang in Tennessee, Missouri, and other places.

Back then however, because I was so small, in school plays, pageants, little womanless weddings (—isn't that name a hoot?) Minstrel shows, and wherever I sang, I was stood on covered tables, pedestals, what have you, so that I could be seen, and heard.

I will never forget, once mother dressed me, and sat me outside on a small bike given to us. People passed, and said what a beautiful child, what a good child.

As I got older I recalled that. Remembering those words, and the ones offered when I sang did not puff me up though, not with pride. They simply let me know that there was something within me. A type of light that was visible, to others. Therefore, I wanted to use that light, in some way, to help others and myself. Back then, pretty was not a weapon to be wielded. Not like it is now. Neither was talent.

Sure, women used it to better their circumstances, just like men used their brawn and money to do so. However, pretty was not as ugly back then as it has become now days, for some. Pretty was as pretty did.

And I had been taught that looks were only skin deep, but ugly was to the bone. That meant—and yet means, for me: that ugly-*actions* were, and are, to be shunned.

*D*REAM ... I often *dreamed* of leaving the places we wound up. Although I was not always aware of it, as I grew, I knew I wanted to leave paralysis, fear, and immobility behind. I also longed for, and dreamed of the right to stand separate from the cotton-field experience.

My dream was to get out of the nightmare of those long six a.m. to six p.m. days. They were days spent in the cotton-fields, with 'stinging worms' and snakes, both of which I was immeasurably afraid.

I despised those cotton fields, the early rising, and planting. I abhorred the task of chopping cotton with the side of that garden tool called a hoe. We did so, to keep the cotton from growing too dense.

Now if I am not explaining it correctly, it is because I never wanted to know these things in the first place.

So … as I was saying, cotton was planted in rows, with no separation. Therefore, it was our job to space it, so that it would grow into stalks. We also had to pull weeds from around it.

This, my family—minus my father whom we had left—did in many a field. That is, until the cotton began to bloom.

Then it became time for picking. To me it seemed that cotton stuff never ended!

Although my siblings and I were children, we too were given long cotton sacks. These hung over our shoulders and we dragged them down the rows. Picking cotton from our left and right, we needed to fill our sacks, in order to get paid at the end of the day.

If we had 100 pounds, then we were perhaps paid a dollar. Perhaps we were cheated, as was often the case.

Out in the cotton fields, from six a.m. until noon we worked, and then had lunch. If we lived nearby, we hurried home to eat previously prepared coldwater cornbread, fashioned in a cast iron black fry pan, with savory beans. If the cotton field wasn't near to home, then we carried lunch and ate beneath whatever shade we could find.

In the sweltering heat, following lunch, we went back to picking cotton. Only to find that sometimes at the end of the day the scale was fixed. However, it was never fixed in our favor.

Most of the time I was the water girl, I guess it was better than picking cotton, with its boll weevils—ugly beetles that fed on the cotton buds as well as flowers.

Jessica Janna & April Alisa Marquette

As the water girl, I had to fetch, fill, and carry a tin pail with a dipper. At a pump, I would pump the water until it got good and cool. This was water from the ground. Then I would walk row by row, giving each worker a cool drink. I made many trips, and everyone drank from the same pail and dipper.

I sometimes got sunspots in my eyes it was so hot out there. I would often see a shimmering, over the fields, as heat rose up and into the atmosphere.

Nowadays, if someone said they saw that, we would rush them to sit. We'd offer them a cold drink, because we would believe they were near heat stroke; but not back then.

Infrequent that the sight was, boy would I be glad to see rain clouds. Yes, because rain would have meant no more dusty, hot, backbreaking work.

Often I would truthfully say that my back hurt. Then most of the adults would tell me that I didn't have a back, not yet, because at the time I was so young.

Sometimes I would wipe a dusty hand over my sweaty brow, beneath my old floppy sunhat. I would *wish* those shadowy rain clouds would ease on over, just a little further. If they did, and brought rain, then we could have stopped work.

However, as it usually happened in the Midwest, the rain clouds were only a tease. Dark and billowing, they would drench the fields just short of us. I would be able to smell the sweet cool, but could not feel it. And I would just want to cry.

Out in those hot fields, bugs, boll weevils, and other kinds of insects, got in my hand-me-down ill-fitting boots. How they did, I will never know, because I wore pants beneath my cotton dress, or overalls. And both were stuffed into my boots.

Armyworms, small and green also got in those boots of mine. The worms turned up, to also eat the cotton, and it seemed that they and the bugs were all over the place.

I was so scared until sometimes I would scream and try to 'dance' those unwanted 'visitors' out of my boots. Out in those fields I always felt icky, jumpy, and panicky.

Yet Mother would quiet me down, so that I could resume my duties.

I got a spanking once, however. I was supposed to chop cotton. Instead I stood, talking. I cannot remember whether I was speaking to myself or to my elder sister. I only know that *she* was smart enough to continue working. So there I was, carrying on a conversation. Wound up getting my butt beat. That got me back to work. However, it did not deter me from dreaming.

My *dream* was to leave that time, that place, and that space … for something better, something more.

Sharecropping

*W*HEN we were yet with my father, we lived in a field, in a house for sharecroppers. This house was small and nothing special. I remember us all sleeping in one room … I am not sure though, if it was there, or elsewhere.

At that old sharecropper house, my father did the plowing for a 'Mr. Boss Man.'

Usually, Father was out until lunch, then he would come home to eat. After lunch, at one p.m., he would go back to the field. In that life of cultivating the soil, Father would stay out until six, or sundown.

It was a hard life. Moreover, there was virtually no way to get ahead. Therefore, by that time, my Father's song was nearly gone. It had been replaced

Jessica Janna & April Alisa Marquette

by alcohol. This replacement made him sullen, and mean, not a joy to be around.

Somehow, as a seedling, I knew that was not the life I wanted. Therefore, I would talk to my little self when things got rough. When Father acted up, I would tell myself there was something or someone out there who would help. They would aid me to leave that hot, dismal place.

A Fight in the Night

*H*OW would you like to wake up to a rat attempting to bite on your feet? Well, from experience, I can tell you, it is no fun.

I believe I was four years old. I told you that at one point my family and I were all crammed together in one room. We, the children slept in one bed, and Mother and Father slept in the other.

We had a charcoal cooker in that room. It was a little round tub that was placed on the floor. Inside it, Mother would put charcoal, and cause them to catch fire. Then she would put a pot, filled with whatever she would cook, on top of those hot coals.

Often rats got in our one room, to poke about for food. My father ran them out, or killed them, whichever came first. These rodent pests also came in to get out of the cold. If they could fit, they entered through holes or cracks in the walls and floor.

Oh were they ugly things, with beady eyes, twitching whiskers, greedy reaching hand-like paws and long hairless tails. Some of those unwanted visitors were also vicious.

Such was the case on the night of which I now speak. A wharf rat entered our domain, and awakened the family. I guess after poking about and finding no food, he decided to make a meal of one of us. Thus, this rat began to nip at someone's toes. I do not remember exactly, but it could have been the baby, Brother, that this rodent went after.

Well, jumping up and getting us some light, my father attempted to remove the ugly gray 'visitor.'

Subsequently, with his teeth bared and his whiskers twitching, the huge rat, bigger than a cat, began to growl. Perhaps he did not want to go.

Up on the bed, screaming and seeking purchase so that we would not fall off, we the children scrambled about. Mother tried to make us hold still. However, neither her words nor her pulling made any difference. All that hissing and growling, as my father chased that rat was truly frightening.

Father used a broom, trying to flatten the ugly beast. However, that only heightened the rat's anger.

By then, I was heaving and crying, because I wanted it all to be over. I wanted my Father up off the floor. I wanted the baby to quit screaming, and I wanted to sleep, in peace.

Mother grabbed an iron, the heavy old-fashioned kind that was often heated on the stove. She heaved it in the direction of that growling rodent. She missed, but not by much.

That creature was getting angrier by the moment.

Jessica Janna & April Alisa Marquette

At one point, my father dashed up on the bed, perhaps to catch his breath.

Then an idea must have struck, because off the bed he darted, leaving us screaming.

Father grabbed what we would today call a fireplace poker. To us it was the utensil used to move the charcoal about in the burner when Mother cooked.

Backing the vicious unwanted visitor into a corner, my father finished that rat off. Using the poker, Father made sure that particular angry creature would never trouble us again.

However, the creature's squeals were nightmarish, and the ensuing scene, of course that had to be cleaned up. And I'm sure you can imagine how frightened we were when our parents had to begin setting things to rights again.

I did not want Mother to move. I certainly did not want Father dragging those hideous remains about, but what had to be done was done.

Crying, I could barely catch my breath. I didn't want to put my feet down. I didn't want the light off, ever again.

I really just wanted a different existence, because as a seedling, I *knew,* no children, or adults, were *supposed* to live that way, having to fight in the night, just to get a little sleep.

Jessica Janna & April Alisa Marquette

Moving & Shaking

*P*REVIOUSLY, I told you there were some things that Mother simply would not stand for. Well the attempted rape of one of her girls was one of those things. I had elder sisters. Their father had passed on. And my father one day got the notion to force himself on one of them.

Well, Ms. Cleo was clearly having none of that! She must have felt as I do. There is just no reason for a grown man to attempt to overpower a girl for his own lustful purposes. It is not right.

You see, often times a man who has very little or no integrity will try this. This type of man sometimes preys on women and women-children.

Perhaps this man feels these women have no recourse. Or maybe the perpetrator feels he can act in an undesirable manner simply because his intended victim is economically at his mercy. The victim(s) may be dependent upon the man for shelter or provision, namely money. Or, in other cases, Mr. Perpetrator may have a need to be 'over' someone. Perhaps economically *he* feels powerless. He may feel he has not received his 'fair share.' Or he feels he has been stepped on. Who knows? We only know there are any number of thought-processes that fuel ugly actions.

Therefore, believing he will inflate himself— believing he will feel larger, Mr. Perpetrator attempts to stick it to others, literally.

This path my father chose. I do not *want* to say this, but I must speak the truth, for it has a way of liberating one.

Yes, we *all* have secrets—skeletons in our closets. However, I believe that the power that these so-called skeletons have over us can be removed.

Jessica Janna & April Alisa Marquette

We must acknowledge our skeletons, our hurtful things. We must be unwilling to hide or cower in the face of them.

Therefore, in refusing to cower, I reveal this torrid ugliness. Perhaps from my revelation, you will gain strength, if needed, to face your skeleton, your demon.

My darling, do not allow ugliness to take precedence in your life. As one who has lived many years, I reiterate, give ugliness no power over you.

And for Lord's sake, forgive! I know, I know, it *is* hard. However, had I lived all these years reliving and mentally replaying all the wrongs done to me, and to those I've loved, I would be merely a shell. I would not be the woman that our Creator designed me to be. I would have thereby given all the ills of my life power over me. However, I am unwilling to do that. I am not willing to live—no, merely exist, rather—in that manner.

As a result, I have become stronger, for letting ugliness go. I try to face that bad things, hurtful things have happened. Yet, *I am here.* I am alive. Therefore, I pray. I ask for grace, and for the God-given strength that will keep me from giving pride of place to ugliness, and hurtful occurrences.

Now ... back to Mother, another thing she would not stand for was a man laying his hands on her, in an abusive manner. This my father also attempted, several times.

Now I told you Mother was a beautiful brown woman. She had an innate grace, and a way about her that made people take notice.

Therefore, if a man tipped his hat to her, or if a male neighbor said as little as "good day," my father became jealous, and unreasonable.

As a child, I heard my parent's rumbles and scuffles. I have vague hazy memories of him lumbering about after he had been drinking. Those sounds scared me, especially when we, the children, were told to hush, to remain quiet. We were to remain unseen and out of the way, so as not to incur wrath.

I also actively recall hearing my father ominously tell Mother, "I will stop your clock..."

Their skirmishes, and muffled scuffles, my mothers little noises, are most likely the reason that I have never been able to stand dissention.

I must admit that although I loved my father, even as a seedling, I knew he was wrong. Real love does not cause one to hurt the very person they claim to love. Real honest-to-goodness love is also not cloying and clutching, or manipulative and controlling.

Real love allows all involved to breathe, and to *be*, freely.

Perhaps, knowing this is why I wrote the song 'Free to be Free' but that I will mention when I recollect older years...

But to get back on track, since my father was proving to be a mini tyrant, Ms. Cleo had us—her children—moving and shaking, again. It seems we moved often during my formative years. However, looking back, I do not regret it. I simply realize that my mother taught us, through her actions, that there were some things we could *not* accept. She taught us to retain our dignity, even if to do so we had to *run*.

So run we did, to catch a train...

*F*OR days and days before we caught our train, we buried clothes, down by the river. Mother had us carry our belongings each day, in clothing wrapped bundles. This she did because she did not want us to leave anything of importance at the sharecropper house once we had departed.

Somewhat superstitious as some southern women are, Mother always believed that were one inclined, that one could do another harm.

My father believed this too, and I vaguely recall some woman he'd run with trying to do my mother harm, so that the woman could have my father.

Anyway, Mother believed harm could be accomplished with a little witchcraft. Yes, with strands of hair, or with articles of clothing that had been worn close to the body of the intended victim.

I know this is why she never wanted laundered under things pegged and hung out on a clothesline, not in plain sight.

Mother used to tell stories of how she had heard that people had done evil. One story went like so...

If a woman became highly upset with another, Miz Upset would get hold of a photo of Another's' baby.

Miz Upset would perform a ritual—work roots. During this ritual, Miz Upset would turn the photo of Another's baby facedown, in the dirt. (Yes, there were photographs when I was young.) Miz Upset would then bury the photo.

Another's baby was supposed to die.

Whether or not the baby died, I do not know. I do know though that for doing evil, people pay. I have lived to see it. Do evil, reap the whirlwind, heap evil back upon your own head.

So back to Mother; believing things could be done to us, through our things, she made us remove all that belonged to us from the house.

I realize, now, that of course she left negligible things, because that lady was nobody's fool.

Jessica Janna & April Alisa Marquette

She left inconsequential things, so that during the days leading up to our departure, our homestead would appear as it always had, so as not to cause alarm.

Yet faithfully, day after day, we walked up a long dusty road, carrying our bundled belongings. We only took what we could carry in our arms because we were on foot.

Now I believe I told you, my father plowed for a 'boss' man. Therefore, my father was out until lunch most days. That was when he came home to eat. Then he was back out again, working until six, sundown or thereabout. Well each day while he was out, we removed clothing, among other things.

Mother was afraid that if she did not leave my father, he would kill her. He had certainly told her as much on occasion. In addition, his jealousy was getting out of hand, as was his drinking.

Looking back, I see that my father had previously been a charmer. In times past he had not shown the cruel side of himself. However, when it became apparent, it was then time to go.

Since Mother feared for her life, and for ours, we were going to Memphis. A friend of hers, Ms. Bretta was going to put us up.

But seemed to me … we had *already been* out to Ms. Bretta's at some point in the past…

Jessica Janna & April Alisa Marquette

The Scariest Day

I will never forget the day we ran away, from home, from my father. We were carrying a few belongings. I was quite young. My brother had been born by then and he was a hip baby.

Affixed to Mother's side, Brother's chubby little hands clutched Mother's clothing as he was jounced along.

As Mother nearly ran up the dusty road toward the station, my short legs propelled me along behind and sometimes beside her.

I very nearly wanted to cry I was so afraid.

Running, I could barely breathe, or see through threatening tears. I really did not understand at the time why we were running, rushing away, but I knew that doing so was of utmost importance.

That, Mother had made clear.

$\mathcal{T}$HE freight train we were to ride on stopped about five or so miles from the sharecropper shack that we'd left behind. This train stopped in a nearby dusty country town, and many times before, I hadn't even been cognizant of hearing it lumber on by, passing through the countryside.

I can remember, all these years later though, that people were yelling, telling us to hurry, hurry.

I was running as fast up that dusty slope as my little legs would carry me, me and the bundle of belongings that I closely clutched.

A man was waving; calling out that the train was a 'coming. And with my heart beating so fast that I felt it would fly right out of my chest, I could barely hear that man.

I did hear someone warningly say though, that we did not want to miss that train.

Jessica Janna & April Alisa Marquette

Obviously, those urging us on knew our plight.
Some probably wanted to aid us to attain safe
passage.

Others possibly wanted to watch, and whisper.

*L*ATER, my father returned from the field. I
know he found silence, and near-empty rooms.

When he smelled nothing cooking, that was most
likely the first giveaway. Then as he walked
through the empty house, I'm sure he suffered from
shock, and then rage, upon realizing that my
mother, her children, and his children were gone.

*H*OWEVER, some time before my father's
arrival home, we—my mother and her children—
had reached our train, just in time.

People aided us. Someone boosted Mother up, as
she held to Brother. That baby clung to her, his

chubby thighs clamped to her hip as she wiggled the fingers of her free hand.

Seeing Mother reach for my sister and I, whom she was not about to leave behind, I felt strong hands vise about my torso. Beneath my arms, those hands lifted me.

Then up on the train I dashed into Mother. I probably almost knocked her down. Frightened beyond all thinking, I also clutched her skirt…

Thus began our ride back to Tomatop Street, where Ms. Bretta awaited.

The Three B's
Bretta, Bubby & Budoo

*I*N Tennessee, there was a cute little white house with latticework around the bottom. The lady of the house was Mother's friend, Ms. Bretta.

Of medium height, Ms. Bretta was fair-skinned and quite boisterous. That fearless woman would put a hand on her hip in a jiffy, and if need be, she would get anyone told!

She had a son, little brown Bubby, who was perhaps four years old at the time. He was my playmate, my friend, my love.

Bubby sang to me. I do not know where he heard this particular song, but he would always sing it… *Ain't I good to You.*

My lovely lisping little Bubby could not pronounce G's, R's, or L's well then, so to me his singing sounded much like 'dee (gee) baby ain't I dood (good) to you. I bought you a diamond wing fuh Chwistmas, and a Cadiwac caw. Dee baby ain't I dood to you...'

It tickles me to this day to recall his sweet singing.

Often when Bubby wasn't singing, he and I would crawl under Ms. Bretta's house. Since it stood on pillars, we could fit, perfectly. We would sit in the cool and peek through the latticework that was like a beautiful skirt surrounding that peaceful home.

*N*OW there was a woman who passed, many days. And Bubby had me frightened of this woman.

Garbed in lengthy black, the woman's head was also always covered in dark cloth (at least whenever we saw her). The woman carried a walking stick, and Bubby would speak in a cautious little voice whenever she passed. He would say that the woman in the dark clothes was the *Budoo Wady*. He meant the Budoo *Lady*.

With rounded eyes, my lovely lisping Bubby would frighten me by telling me that the Budoo Wady was going to get me. As if I did not already have enough in my young life to be frightened of.

Once, that woman noticed Bubby and I beneath Ms. Bretta's house. I don't know what she thought we were doing, but The Budoo Lady turned and shook her walking stick at us.

She had to know that Bubby and I were awed by, and afraid of her, as we shrank back.

Thinking back on it, I am sure Bubby and I were a sight, peering from beneath that house as the Budoo Lady swished on past.

On Our Trail

*O*NE evening I was playing in Ms. Bretta's yard.
Mother had taken in some washing and ironing,
which she did, to make money. In addition to
feeding us, she had to pay Ms. Bretta. She could not
stay on the woman, using up her kindness, for free.
So stopping work for the day, Mother called me
inside.

On this particular evening, Bubby must have
been away, visiting, because I recall being alone
when Mother called. Afterward, a strange thing
happened...

My father walked up. I was confused. To me, it
seemed he had gotten there too fast. I wondered
why, what could have made him think to arrive
there of all places. As an adult, I now know that any
one of numerous things could have been the catalyst
for his appearance.

Jessica Janna & April Alisa Marquette

In the house, my mother and Ms. Bretta scurried to quietly get us into hiding. Then Ms. Bretta stepped outside her home.

Showing his congenial self, my father bid her a good evening. It seems many people do not do that any more. However, because he could be charming when he chose, we heard my father do so.

"Hey Ms. Bretta," I remember him calling out. "Have you seen my wife?"

In the house, we could not see Father from our hiding place in the back. However, hearing him was truly terrifying. In addition, knowing what he was capable of when he had been angered caused the shakes.

Also knowing that Ms. Bretta told an untruth, to protect our lives, was doubly frightening.

"No, no," she called in response, "I ain't seen Cleo."

Well we listened to Ms. Bretta and my father's exchange. With pounding heart, I know Mother prayed that my small brother would remain quiet.

Out of doors, in the drawing dusk, my father proceeded to tell Ms. Bretta that my mother had left him—and had taken the children.

Ms. Bretta did a bit of acting, caught in the middle as she was.

I guess my father couldn't help himself. He got a little heated. Most likely in a message for my mother, he went on to ominously say that she had better not let him catch her…

Now the Lord knows only a *true* friend would step between a woman and harm. And that night that is what Ms. Bretta did, proving to be Mother's true friend.

Following that harrowing episode, my mother had to hurriedly put her little money together, to get her children back to Pine Bluff, Arkansas.

Jessica Janna & April Alisa Marquette

Mother decided we would go back to Arkansas, because should my father look for us there, he would go to jail. In Pine Bluff, he had jumped bail. There he had been charged with the legal term for being abusive, and for the attempt on my sister.

Since my father had a history there, Mother knew he would never go back.

*T*HAT night when sleep should have come, fear skulked heavily about.

A man, Ms. Bretta's cousin also slept in the house that night, quite possibly for our protection. However, each time I awoke with a start and heard his awful, loud snoring, I became frightened all over again.

For crying aloud, the man sounded like he was howling in a tin can.

THE very next day, with help from Mother's friend, we boarded another train.

Anxious to help, Ms. Bretta pressed money on my mother and saw us safely aboard.

I know she prayed, as we went clacking down those railroad tracks, back to Pine Bluff.

I remember crying, off and on, all day long when Mother first took me to school.

Kindergarten marked my first time really being away from Mother. And it was terrible, for me.

Mamas sometimes think it is traumatic for them to be away from a small child, but trust me; it is just as heart wrenching for the child. However, we all get along.

It is the way of life. We move, we change and we grow.

I went to bigger school the next year, and I was over the crybaby stage. That year our family also attended the Presbyterian Church. Mother took us.

She wore her patent leather shoes, and her dark skirt and white blouse. My, did she look lovely. She always was a shapely little thing.

Funny, I cannot remember if the people in the church were white or black (*my daughter asked*). I did not see color then. I simply knew that I liked church. I loved the singing. I loved the feeling that rose inside me, like a huge happy bubble that wanted to fly me right up to heaven.

As visitors, that first time, we had to stand, to be recognized.

During those years, it seemed we were always moving. We never stayed any place for long. However, Mother took us to many churches, Methodist, Catholic, Pentecostal…

WE attended one school where there was a girl, a bully. My sister, the bookworm mentioned her. Sister said, "The kids think you're afraid of Bully."

I was not afraid, I was just not thinking about Bully.

Jessica Janna & April Alisa Marquette

Well, Bully made me think about her. One day she got all up in my face, after she'd put a chip on her shoulder—an actual small piece of wood!

With children jostling all about, she tried to prod me. She dared me to knock the chip off her.

I thought that was the dumbest thing. Yet, I finally got sick of Bully, her taunting, and all the noise and pushing from the other schoolchildren.

Therefore, I did what Bully wanted. I knocked the chip off her shoulder. I knocked some chips out of her too!

Funny, then my sister was filled with pride. She talked about it all the way home. She told others they should have seen. "Jessie tore bully up!"

$\mathcal{B}$ACK then, in the early 1940's Hitler was in power. Occasionally, in the states there were blackouts. Then we children ran around in the street. We would whisper, scratchily, that we were not ever to speak of him. For even we knew, that man was truly evil personified.

*M*OTHER moved us from Memphis to Kiwanis. When we went to Missouri, Mother left my elder sister with a woman called Miss Mary. She did so because of the attempted rape by my father.

Another sister was not with us either. She had been forced to marry an old guy. Or perhaps he just seemed that way to me, since I was so young. I remember Sister had to go with him, even though he was toting a gun. She had only been thirteen at the time.

As a child, I felt bad. I could not put all my feelings together, but I knew the situation did not feel right, or good.

Mother had been coerced into believing those arrangements would be better for her older girls than continuously fighting off the advances of men.

Jessica Janna & April Alisa Marquette

My darling, anyone who believes that mothers do not have to make the hardest choices, needs to speak to a few. These mothers will explain and dismiss doubt, and many times through tears.

I do believe that was one of the hardest things my mother had to do, to let her girls go.

As a result, one of my sisters said—in later years—that *I* was the beloved child, because Mother kept me with her.

I know though, that Mother kept me, and baby brother, because we were too young. Like any true mother, she would not have willingly separated from any of her children, were it not for their good.

Mother did get my sister back, when we became more settled, when we were without my father. Then when I sang in school, my sister wound up enduring the teasing of children who were amused by my pronunciation in song. That I mentioned before.

As small as I was, I could also be mean.

People in school didn't know it, but I will never forget … I stabbed my sister's arm with a butcher knife. I did so because she reached for something on my plate. I think it may have been cornbread.

As you can well imagine, I got my ornery little butt beat, torn up in fact.

Mother established boundaries with that whupping. She made me understand that using knives and weapons was not to be in our family. She said that as siblings, we were not to fight each other, and especially not over food.

Mother truly gave me what-for with a switch— probably one that she told *me* to go pull off a small tree or bush. I never forgot the stinging, or the accompanying lesson.

Jessica Janna & April Alisa Marquette

*O*H I need to tell you, and do not laugh. There was a man, I don't know if he lived nearby, but he was sometimes out and about.

People said he preached in the surrounding area. I sure hope not; because he would walk through the cornfields, wearing a coat. There was nothing wrong with that; but beneath his coat this man wore nothing. Passing through the tall stalks, one could hear rustling as he walked. Doing so, he would open his coat—and flash people—gave them a glimpse of his nudity.

Though his actions were messy, people generally forgave him—since he never harmed anyone…

Honey, I mentioned it, so I could tell you: that's something we've got to do in this life. We must forgive. *And* I pray that man found his clothing.

Meet E G

$\mathcal{S}$OMEHOW, we wound up in Moscow. There, Mother met another woman named Mary. In time, this Mary introduced Mother to a tall handsome man named E G. Whew! Was he a looker. He caught eyes and turned female heads everywhere he went.

Mary, older than Mother, urged her to take up with E G. Mary said E G was the marryin' kind.

I know sometime later, after I had been in school a good while, Mother wound up indeed marrying E G. In those days, weddings were not the big staged productions that they are now. You said your vows, you prayed, you got married. Then you went back to work.

Honeymoon? (*My daughter asked.*) What was that—in those days? There was not time to lay up, touching and such. All that came when the day's work was done, after supper, chores, and prayers.

Anyway, the small ceremony was at the house. I seem to recall that Mother had on a blue dress. I do not even recollect if anyone outside the family attended.

I do know that we did not have food like people do now, all the lavish buffets. There was no reception. I do not remember whether Mother took off the blue dress and went back to the field either...

It has been sixty-some odd years since then, so how can I remember every single detail? However, I recall that back then, as a child, I was only interested in playing, and how not to go to the field.

Grandmaw

*W*E met Grandmaw, E G's mother. People said she was Indian—however, today we know that she was Native American. She had long black hair to her waist, creamy bisque-colored skin, and coal black eyes.

Sometimes Grandmaw would comb her hair out, from the one braid, or the two that she often wore. Then, to me all that hair would look like a huge black cloud.

In our new existence, Mother cooked, cleaned, and was the general help all around—just like many women today. Papa E worked on the railroad. And Grandmaw was just the resident pain in my neck.

Each day Mother got up early, cooked breakfast, fed her husband, Grandmaw, and us.

Jessica Janna & April Alisa Marquette

Mother also prepared dinner, which today would be called lunch, and then supper, whilst she did her many other chores.

$\mathcal{I}$ went to elementary school. I recall it had a fancy name. There the teachers were nice, they loved me, but they were not thorough. Perhaps the thought-process back then was that we, the children, were not going to have much use for education in our adult lives. I sure hope that was not the case.

Anyway, those teachers loved my singing, but they were not very skilled, and could not truly communicate the essence or the value of learning to their charges.

Subsequently, I felt cheated somehow, and stupid, because I knew I was not getting what I needed. I don't know how I knew, but within I truly felt this. Therefore, instead of reading, I listened and memorized. I did so, for many reasons. One of them was so that my sister who had to help me with my homework could hurriedly get back to whatever book she wanted to read.

Well one day in school, I was called on to read something. I did ... but I did not realize I had the book upside down.

My teacher caught on to me. She did not make me feel bad. She simply acknowledged that I had to be very smart. Yes, indeed, to go to all the trouble of memorization and reciting, just to keep from reading.

Silly me, I simply wanted 'being put on the spot' to be over. That was how I saw it.

Jessica Janna & April Alisa Marquette

In Moscow

I told you we met Grandmaw, E G's mother. Her husband, E G's father, had been a black man. It is said he was rich and had many acres of land.

Therefore, Grandmaw also owned property in Pine Bluff. However, after Mother and E G's marriage, Mother took us, the children, to go live with E G and Grandmaw.

Sometimes Grandmaw was … well *different*, to me. She had a way of looking seemingly through a person, with her knowing dark eyes. She often spoke her mind as well. Although I was little, things Grandmaw said hurt my feelings, or really got on my nerves.

Seemed like she was always bothering me... I felt like she was constantly saying something, to me, or about me. She said I was too pretty. She said I was lazy. Sometimes she said I was mean. She also said

I was not going to do anything but grow up and bring Cleo a pack of babies.

I knew I would one day prove her wrong.

I know I got on her nerves too, because in a way, I was just like her. I spoke my mind, at times.

It was probably why once when I got a spanking from Mother; black-eyed Grandmaw goaded her on, glad that I was getting it.

I probably could have taken that same switch to Grandmaw.

$\mathscr{A}$T the new (to us) four-room house of E G and Grandmaw, there was a lot of junk. The house was like an old barn, with a porch straight across the front. Now on this long porch were old cushioned chairs. There were also used tires in a pile on one end—an ugly sight, I know.

In the sweltering heat, I would sit on the porch, on my little rug; not really taking notice of the Lazy Susan's whose faces were upturned to the hot sun.

Some days, to pass the time, my baby brother and I sat on that long porch and named the cars that passed on the highway before the house.

Other times my little brother would name all the farm animals. He said Ducky Lucky, Cowdy Dowdy, and many more were his friends. Now, the funny thing is, there was no TV, so where brother got the names I did not know. They just came to him as I babysat him. And because I took care of him, people started calling me lil Mama.

*M*OTHER spent a lot of time cleaning and emptying those junky rooms.

When we first moved into E G and Grandmaw's house, there was always something cooking on the stove. To me, whatever it was smelled curdled, and rank. Mother soon made all gone of that though, when *she* began meal preparations.

Living there, I got my first taste of turtle meat. I tell you it was different. Grandmaw cooked it, and bragged about how inside the turtle there was every kind of meat. She said you could taste pork, beef, venison, and chicken. I figured; why not just eat the other meat then? If you could get hold of it; why make-believe with the poor turtle?

It was then that I decided, turtle meat, turtle soup, and or turtle stew, none of that was for me.

Before Grandmaw was 'relieved' of her cooking duties, she also made very bad, big biscuits. We, the kids, called them 'cat-head' biscuits. Do not ask me why. And no, those things were not what I knifed my sister for, when I got that stinging whupping.' I fought her over Mother's cornbread.

On the Moscow farm, there were many children's chores. There was milking to be done.

The chickens and the pigs had to be fed. Home fires needed to be started in the pot-bellied heaters, and the wood-burning stove.

Pretty Baby

OH, the baby. I nearly forgot to tell you about her…Yet whenever I think of her, it is with such vivid clarity.

In time, after mother married E G, she wound up with child.

As a child myself, I knew we were going to have a new addition to the family. I had also heard it said, after a while, 'that baby should have been here by now.'

Well, when the baby was finally born, she was absolutely beautiful. Mother had the pretty baby at home, but … something seemed wrong. I could tell. Perhaps it was the absence of joy, and the fact that there was whispering.

As I peeked, the midwife handled Pretty Baby. Oh was she a living doll!

Jessica Janna & April Alisa Marquette

Fully formed and round, she had a lot of black curly hair. The baby, whom I will call Pretty, also appeared rosy.

She looked like a two or three month old as well ... *but* she was not moving.

That was strange, to me. She did not even cry. It seemed the midwife could not elicit a sound out of Pretty, who simply looked to be sleeping, amid all the hurrying about and hush-hush as Mother lay abed, sobbing.

Then one of the neighbor women perhaps, said what no one wanted to say.

Pretty was dead.

It was a shock to hear. And it was hurtful, I felt a kind of anger as from my corner out of the way, I watched while that beautiful doll baby was dressed and laid upon the bed.

Oh, we admired Pretty, when we no longer had to lurk in the hallway.

Beyond the bedroom, with E G, we had heard Mother's screams, and the coaching, all the sounds that made one's heart race.

Therefore, when at last we were allowed in, Mother was somewhat unlike Mother. As she bore the silent stares, she suffered from what I now know was grief.

I heard old forever-talking Grandmaw too, *again*. She said, "Cleo you should not have been pulling up into that back do'."

Like Pretty's death had been my mother's fault! I wanted to rush over to Grandmaw and bite her on the leg, or pummel her good.

How else, I had thought, was my mother going to get into the rear of the house, after she had been outside at that washtub, doing laundry? She'd had to get back inside, to do other chores. Among them, she'd had to feed forever-talking, sometimes trouble-making Grandmaw.

Jessica Janna & April Alisa Marquette

Anyway, *Grandmaw's son*, Papa E had not gotten around to fixing the steps yet. He had been working, so Mother had only done what she'd had to, to maintain home and hearth—without complaint.

When night fell, it was suggested that 'this particular midwife'—who had gone by then—had not known what to do for Pretty. It was whispered that someone should have told Midwife, or she should have known to suck the mucous from Pretty's nose. Then mayhap Pretty could have been jumpstarted into breathing.

However, by that time it was too late. It had been too long.

Pretty was put into a little box, a tiny coffin. Where it came from, I do not know.

Amid the angst and pain, someone suggested that Mother had carried Pretty too long. It was said that Pretty was most likely supposed to have been born some time before. Oh, a heap of things were tossed and bantered about, stupid, tactless stuff. Not very many of those words were comforting. None of them made me feel any better, because I *wanted* Pretty.

Mother wanted her baby too. *I* wanted that beautiful baby alive. I did not want her lying on Mother's bed, or lying fully dressed and in that box, like a lovely doll.

I wanted Mother to tend Pretty. I wanted things to be right, but they could not, because everything was all wrong. Though I didn't know it at the time, all of that hurt. It hurt like I couldn't breathe, although being so young, I did not recognize that hurt as pain, or as the grief that it was.

There was a funeral, for Pretty. Prayers were said. There was wailing and crying, and the beautiful baby was buried. It was traumatic.

I was miserable, my head hurt, along with my heart.

Mother was distraught.

Back then, I knew Pretty would leave us. Living that life so close to the earth; to the soil, and to farm animals, I had seen death, and a lot of it. I knew that once death came, whatever or whoever had been alive would be gone, forever.

I did not want Pretty gone. I wanted to hold her, to tend her, like I had done brother, who did not need me as much anymore. I wanted to one day hear Pretty's baby gurgle and giggles. I wanted to teach her to clap her chubby beautiful little hands. But now, none of that would ever be.

IN time, Mother returned to being Mother. She even wound up with child again. But I never forgot. Pretty has stayed with me, in my mind and heart ever since the day that she came into our lives, just before she went back out again.

She was the beautiful candle, whose light flickered for just moments, and then it was gone. However, she is not gone. She has never been, not for me.

Moreover, while Mother lived, for her, Pretty Baby was never gone. As the mother that I am today, I know that, with all my heart.

Jessica Janna & April Alisa Marquette

.*I*N Moscow, as in any town, there were characters. One in particular was a man, dubiously called Dandy Boy. This ne'er do well and his twin brother were considered the town clown-outs. Often hanging about in jook joints, it seemed Dandy Boy's activities were often suspect.

I had not known him, because at the time, I was a child. However, I'd heard people, E G and others, mention Dandy Boy. I cannot tell you that E G or others were very fond of this particular man.

What I can say is that one night Mother put her children to bed. Some time later, while we lay quiet, there came a knock on our door.

A man stood outside our home, speaking. His words immediately worried Mother. Thus, she hurriedly readied herself to take a short ride.

Unaware then, Mother had been told an untruth. However, because E G, her husband was out, this fabrication, this lie, seemed plausible.

Therefore, as a lamb led to the slaughter, Mother allowed the man who turned out to be Dandy Boy to coerce her into leaving home. Of course, Grandmaw was yet in the house, to make sure no harm came to us, the children.

Out of doors, Mother was escorted to Dandy Boy's automobile. We later found out that this vile man had told Mother that E G was just up the road apiece. Believing E G had suffered illness or an attack—I do not know which—Mother rode with Dandy Boy.

Some time later, there was great commotion at our home. Mother was back, but was she a sight!

Jessica Janna & April Alisa Marquette

Shaking, and wild-eyed, her clothing was torn and dirty. Her hair had brambles in it, and she was no doubt bruised and sore from having to fight. Just seeing her this way, and hearing all the hubbub was most frightening for us, the children.

In the hustle and bustle, the chaos and confusion, it became known that Dandy Boy had attacked Mother. When he had gotten her a ways from the house, he'd pushed her from his automobile. In a field, he set about to pounce upon her and have his way with her.

Although she was a little thing, Mother had put up a mighty fight. If she was going to be accosted, she must have decided, she would not go down like a ten-pin. All this information came out as neighbors, quite a few of them angry males, pressed into our home.

E G, who had been out selling moonshine—
homemade distilled corn liquor—his 'second job'
his moonlighting gig, was then summoned.

It appeared that Dandy Boy had gotten the
foolish notion to do what he had, because perhaps
he had seen E G in passing. Perhaps this vile man
had deduced that Mother, lovely to look at, was at
home without her man. Whatever his thought
process, things did not bode well for the fool called
Dandy Boy.

When E G raced up, he was veritable cauldron of
rage. Anger blazed in his eyes. Although he tried to
contain himself, to find out from Mother what had
happened, he fairly simmered, one degree from
boiling.

Retrieving his shotgun, E G slammed out of the
house. Others clattered after him, calling and

slamming automobile and truck doors. They too wanted a piece of the man who had dared to put his hands on my mother, Ms. Cleo.

E G did not have to search long for his prey, whom he found cowering somewhere beneath the darkened sky. I am told that Dandy Boy was so frightened, that his eyes glittered like a small animal's in the night.

Tearing out of his truck with his shotgun, E G called to the man he would surely kill. He roared that Dandy Boy should come from crouching, and face his fate like a man.

When Dandy Boy did not, E G, in full rage, tore open his shirt while holding his gun aside. He growled at the other man, giving him a chance to do his worst, to a *man*.

Yet Dandy Boy cowered. Then he did what to those gathered was amazing. He tore out running!

Everyone present, and at home knew one thing. Nothing could outrun a bullet from E G.

At home, when E G returned, with love all in his eyes for precious Mother, things began to settle down.

However, the events of that evening became a lesson. They also became part of the legend of E G in those parts: Only a *fool* would fool with what belonged to that man.

I heard that way later, in town, when he finally came out of hiding, Dandy Boy's path intersected with E G's. Having barely escaped with his life, the younger male made it a point to steer clear. Forever more he kept his distance, from the man, and woman whom he should never have crossed to begin with.

Jessica Janna & April Alisa Marquette

E G had sons, and daughters. They were a good deal older than my siblings and I. They were from a previous union involving E G.

He had one daughter in particular. This one was a little older than I was. I remember her because she used to come for the summers. She and I would play together. I knew she came to be with her father, but I felt she came for me. We were friends, and I was somewhat in awe of her.

This little girl had the most beautiful clothes, the likes of which my sisters and I did not have. I was not jealous, but Grandmaw made me angry, whenever my little friend visited.

E G's daughter had colorful little suitcases, and gazing upon her, Grandmaw would thoughtlessly remark.

"She's got a mother *and* a daddy."

Grandmaw would look at me. "What you got? Just a wore out ol' piece of mammy."

That hurt. Again, I wanted to fight Grandmaw. I wanted to tear her in two.

Back then, I would forget her words, momentarily. Yet I have never forgotten E G's child. She was like a small prima donna, one that my mother had to take care of for a couple of months each summer.

*T*HEN there was a cousin, we called her Big Baby J. She was a little mess.

Big Baby J was conniving.

When we the children were given candy, BBJ would wait a while. Then she would pretend that all her candy was gone.

I got wise to her though, because after a time or two of this stunt, I noticed something. BBJ would tear through *my* candy and my brother's like a little storm. She would eat up every piece she could get her paws on.

Then she would slyly smile, and bring her own candy out from behind her back.

Did she share with us? No BBJ did not. That was how she was, and she could not see where she was wrong, slick, or selfish.

I thank Big Baby J though, because dealing with her quickly enabled me to see people. I can now see them as they are, and not as the people that they sometimes project.

$\mathcal{I}$told you E G and Grandmaw owned property in Pine Bluff. Therefore, E G had a family house built, while we were living in Moscow.

One day we moved to the new house. Back to Arkansas we went, saying good-bye. No more Moscow, with its forever fields, pitch-dark, and singing night creatures. And no more meddling' Grandmaw—yaaay!

$\mathcal{S}$OON after however, E G moved Grandmaw to Pine Bluff, to be with the family—with us. Ugh!

Although Grandmaw was different, strange even, some said, Mother had the ability to get along with anyone, perhaps because Mother was soft-spoken. She was also easy to entreat, and never did she hold grudges. I think she was too busy. She was also always way too busy to participate in gossip. I never remember her using words to tear anyone down.

Jessica Janna & April Alisa Marquette

Therefore, Mother and Grandmaw did fine. Those two got on well. They even shared the making of our school clothes by hand, often using flour sacks.

Back in those days, huge amounts of flour came in large fabric bags that had floral patterns on them. I remember field flowers and other pastoral scenes. Flour was a staple then, because for us meat was not consumed in the portions that it is now.

In Pine Bluff, again I found myself using the wondrous gift of song, in shows and at church.

Thus began the odyssey of wonderment that would become my life...

I Never Forget...

I always remember my mother's prayers. Often she prayed while busy. She rose early each day, to march around and create order and beauty.

Mother had a thin soprano voice. Hitting high notes, she sang of her God, and of His wonders. Always up early, and working until late, she taught us The Ten Commandments.

Mother took us to different churches. In every city or township that we found ourselves, she found a church. There my spirit was touched. And something within me rose, to meet the something without that reached down to me.

I will never forget her ankle-wrap patent pumps—yes, they had them back then. I remember when her hair was lengthy, dark, and her crowning glory.

Jessica Janna & April Alisa Marquette

My hair she would braid. I would sit on the floor between her knees, or in a chair, with her behind me.

She would brush and comb, and oil my scalp. Despite her loving attention, I never liked those braids, plaits they were sometimes called. Still, she would pat me when she was done, as if my hair and I were her masterpiece.

I would voice my disappointment. I did not want those braids. I wanted my hair like hers.

She would shush me. Often she told me that people thought I was beautiful. Never a woman of many words, she let me know there was a place in the universe that was all mine.

She also taught me prayers, small, seemingly childish, innocuous prayers; *but* because of her, her *words*, those seemingly small offerings, a seed of faith was born in me.

Due to my mother's words, I knew that I could become something.

If you are a mother or any type of caregiver, never forget that *your* words hold power. Many times, your words will lock or unlock doors in the lives of your children, and in the lives of others with whom you speak.

I also want to tell you that at different times during my life, I have felt as if I were in a churn, being broken, tossed, turned, driven, made, and molded. However, because of that tiny seed of faith, which my mother instilled in me, I always knew Spirit would carry me.

I knew, even in my youngest years, my seedling years, that I would get out, that I would have a different life.

Back then, I did not consider this *knowing* faith. It was just something that I knew.

Jessica Janna & April Alisa Marquette

I could not possibly see where I was going, where life, with all its twisting and windings, would take me. However, I knew...

There is a scripture in the bible, Hebrews 11:1, it says *now faith is the substance of things hoped for, the evidence of things not seen.*

That I have learned to live by ... I have believed and tried to follow Spirit—God's rules for loving and not acting ugly. His laws for believing there is more. And in my life it has been proven—there is *more.* Sure, I have been up, living well.

Then I fell, all the way down, went crashing to the ground; but *Spirit* was *always* there.

It is what has kept me moving, and growing, and glowing, despite terrible trials. Those I will later tell you about.

However, for now, just know that if others have hurt or abused *you,* or if you feel unworthy... If you have been dashed, and are currently on your knees, remember. God uses the strangest people. Sometimes even the ones who seem no good. He sometimes uses those who do not even seem smart.

I told you some of what Grandmaw said about me. I also mentioned that sometimes I did not feel smart, but rather simple. Other times I was afraid. I felt hurt, humiliated, and alone.

Therefore, you know I know.

You may feel inferior, or you may have negative emotions and other maladies beating you down; but pick your precious self up. Dust off, and dear baby, run, if you must ... because you too are a seedling— waiting to grow, just as I was.

Jessica Janna & April Alisa Marquette

Salutation

*O*h my dear departed mother Cleopatra... It is on your shoulders that I stand.

Single-handedly, you walked away from abuse, a relationship gone wrong. You did so in the 1940's when this was rarely done. Divorce was not popular then. We knew of no active women's liberation movement at that time. Yet you, sweet Mother, chose to liberate yourself, and your children.

Yes, you were afraid. I remember. You were more aware though, that remaining in an abusive relationship would most definitely affect your children's choices in life. Therefore, you planned, waited, and then you bravely fled—(an oxymoron, I know) with your children in tow.

You dear mother, worked days in people's homes, caring, laundering, cleaning, and cooking for them.

Jessica Janna & April Alisa Marquette

When allowed, you brought treats home to your children.

You took pride in sending us to school. You were proud to care for us, to teach us what little you knew. You felt that we reflected you. Although you were not overly affectionate; did not have time to be, you were proud, of us, of loving us.

Although you did not say it either, not in many words, you wanted so much for us.

I remember, Mama Cleo...In my life I have had many journeys. I have moved from township to township, from city to city, and from state to state. However, if I learned anything from you, dear Mother, it was that I could always be strong, yet never lose the softness that makes me woman.

I have never regretted being your daughter. The effects of your choices, your life, your teachings, your joyous little song in the mornings, has given me pride. You instilled in me respect, and dignity.

I, Jessie, salute you. I do so—even now, after all these years, for the love you showed. You made imprints upon my life, and on the lives of my children—my daughter April especially. I now see much of *you* in her.

Thank you dear Cleopatra, for the love that ever remains. Thank you for teaching me to revere beauty, and life.

Flowers, colors, the scents of country woods, the sound of flowing streams, and fragrant smoke from burning leaves, all of these remind me of you. Hot buttered biscuits, custard pies, family gatherings, someone entering the back door, calling 'yoo-hoo;' a pot of beans, laughter, a porcelain pitcher, a lovely poem…all the simple things that make life worth living, these you taught me to cherish…and I greatly honor you.

Your daughter forever,

Jessie

Jessica

*Greatly desiring to see thee, being mindful of
thy tears, that I may be filled with joy;*

*When I call to remembrance the unfeigned faith
that is in thee, which dwelt first in thy grandmother,
and thy mother... I am persuaded that [this dwells]
in thee also.*

*For God has not given us a spirit of fear but of
power and of love and of a sound mind.*

II Timothy 1:4, 5, 7 [KJV paraphrased]

Email
Jessica Janna
or
April Alisa Marquette
www.aprilalisamarquette.com

Please use the 'Contact Us' page.

To book Jessica Janna for speaking
engagements email:

Lola R. at abusco12@att.net

————————— * —————————

And…for another glimpse into her life, look for:

Sowing

Jessica Janna
&
April Alisa Marquette

Non-Fiction

The second install in the
Relinquish & Reap Series

Thought provoking and poignant…you may laugh or cry as you look into Jessica's life.

Six purse-sized books offer practical wisdom. Each will make you feel as if a lovely friend is telling you her irrepressible story.

Then— Jessica's seventh, an engrossing full-sized volume, will tie all together…

———————— * ————————

Sowing

The Increasing Years

Jessica Janna
&
April Alisa Marquette

As an adolescent and a teenager, Jessica winds up far from home. She is now estranged from her Mother and everything that was once familiar. Sometimes tearful and afraid, Jessica has good reason to feel alone…

Sowing is the **second** account in the true-life inspirational *Relinquish & Reap* Series.

Available 2010
April Rain Books

———————*———————

Desire good fiction?

Glimpse the character inspired by ***Jessica Janna***.

Read about *the Priestess*
in the mysterious, erotic supernatural thriller...

Exodus

by
April Alisa Marquette

Enjoy the following excerpt:

$\mathcal{T}HAT$ night Aqua left Noel's bed. Amid incessant whispers urging her on, she floated, up the small narrow staircase, to the third floor bath.

This time the door was not stuck. Partially open, familiar children's laughter floated out.

It seemed she had heard the airy giggles many times before. But hadn't … she—or someone, *killed* the children?

As she glided forward, her feet never seeming to touch the floor, Aqua's heartbeat quickened. With her hand on the brass knob, she peered inside, and saw two golden haired babes. Perhaps they were three year-olds, but they could have been four.

They had halos of spiral curls; and splashing and laughing, their little faces beamed like sunshine. Their butter colored skin was smooth, stretched taught over curvy little arms, legs, and unblemished backs.

When they turned their heads, yet giggling, Aqua saw their little button noses and lush lips.

Then one child pivoted to look at her, and Aqua wondered, where these children bi-racial? Slowly, the other child also faced her, and she squinted. What color were their eyes?

They were…amber. No green. Wait. Were they gray?

Unable to tell, Aqua moved forward. Suddenly she screamed, and backed up, because the children's eyes were actually hollowed-out sooty *sockets*!

Tickled at her distress, the little ones turned, to face away…

Exodus...

NOW

Available
April Rain Books

www.aprilalisamarquette.com
barnesandnoble.com
amazon.com

———————— * ————————

Then…

April Alisa Marquette does it again…

If you enjoyed visiting The Isle and meeting the High Priestess, in Aqua and Noel's tale—*Exodus* then take a trip.

Rejoin the priestess, and those surrounding her, in:

Affinity

The second install of the Sea Isles Series, a trilogy.

Bon Voyage!

Available 2010
April Rain Books

www.ingramcontent.com/pod-product-compliance
Lightning Source LLC
Chambersburg PA
CBHW020950030426
42339CB00004B/26

* 9 7 8 1 6 1 5 3 9 5 7 2 9 *